Spiritual Feedings

Thoughts
Prayers
Minute Meditations

Anonymous G.

DEDICATION

This book is dedicated to all those who came before me, all those who walk with me, and all those who are yet to come.

I am grateful to all those who touched my heart on my spiritual journey and my hope is these writings may touch your heart on your spiritual journey.

There are just too many people to name here who deserve credit in the making of these Spiritual Feedings, Daily Thoughts, Prayers and Minute Meditations. I am sure I would be remiss and I know I would forget someone. You all know who you are and I thank you for all your help, input, and love.

Most importantly I want to thank God without whose grace, guidance, direction and love none of this would be possible.

Anonymous G.

Spiritual Feedings is a guide and companion for daily living; borrowed from various philosophies, religious beliefs, practices, spiritual doctrines, truths, recovery programs and psychiatry. Use this book as a daily guide in your own individual quest for meanings, truths, clarity, thoughts, calmness, support, ideas, guidance, inspiration, strength, insights, values, tranquility, and understanding on your spiritual journey of growth.

When we are spiritually in the flow of life we effortlessly are in the right place at the right time with the right people.

As we experience more of these spiritual moments, connections, and blessings any number of possibilities await us.

The blessing we find is that we are part of the divine flow of life and the greater good when we are spiritually connected.

Nice place to be!

Every day is a day we can count our blessings and all those things that are special to us.

These things, events, situations, people, and circumstances are sent to wake our spirit.

They show us how to live, be happy, joyous, and free.

Our job becomes to see, remember, and to do what they are telling us.

God makes that awareness possible and we can't do it without His help!

Only I can take the first step to move forward.

It may look or be hard but it is not impossible.

I can ask God for the strength to move forward.

Unless I take action and move forward with God I will never be free of the bondage of self!

How many friends do you have?

Never underestimate how close your friends are and how much love there is for you to give.

Because friendship is all about – loving unconditionally!

It is important to walk our talk.

Not through words but through actions.

That's where integrity is found!

Today I am where I want to be in my life.

Thank you all for teaching me how to live!

Each day we see life's positives and negatives.

If we choose to live in the negative then that is what we will experience.

If we choose to live in the positive then that is what we will experience.

The choice is ours.

We are the only ones who can choose how we look at life.

When experiencing doubts or fears some tools you can use to overcome them are: prayer and share.

They work!

With prayer and meditation as a guide - take action and seek Gods will –a better quality of life will emerge.

Be fearless give God all your negative thoughts, beliefs, actions, and attitudes.

Now relax and watch how God changes your heart and life.

Have you ever noticed that your feelings constantly change?

Have you ever noticed that your life is in a state of flux?

Have you ever noticed that your peace comes from God?

Then you noticed perseverance, adaptability, and love at work!

My attitude can be negative and destructive and that is what I will become.

My attitude can be grateful and loving and that is what I will become.

My attitude determines my actions and my actions determine the results of my life.

Today I can make a choice in my attitude thanks to God's grace and mercy and the help of others!

When we surrender completely to God in faith He will give us what we need.

He may even change our whole existence and the way we live.

It may not be what we want but it is what we need to draw closer to Him.

How do I know this?

Because it happened to me and many, many others and is still happening right now.

Just take the time to stop look around and see His wonders that be!

God comes to anyone who needs, seeks, wants, and is willing to accept Him.

May I get out of the way so that God may enter?

I pray that I may surrender myself to God's power and presence!

Day by day we plant seeds.

That's what we do.

The results are up to God not me or you!

Dealing with our faults and imperfections we are dealing with being human.

We realize every person is growing no matter how faulty or imperfect they might be just as we are growing.

We see how closely we are tied together with our fellows.

We come to accept the idea that no person will ever achieve perfection.

We can look at the faults of others and see our own through them.

Since we are not perfect we learn to be responsible and accountable for our actions and behaviors.

This dealing with being human becomes our spiritual quest and shows our spiritual growth!

While the wait for guidance from God may seem impossible because of self-will.

May I stay focused on God's guidance and will in this moment and not go off on my own.

God help me stay focused so that the impossible becomes possible as I practice waiting in patience on your guidance and will and not mine!

People are put on our path to help us, teach us, and guide us along.

But the lessons to be learned are always ours!

When we are in conflict we become inappropriate, judgmental, critical, misguided, unsupportive, and negative.

With guidance, prayer and meditation, we discover the truth about our conflicts.

The truth is - we are self centered and not God centered.

The solution is - we need Gods help to get us out of self!

Repeating positives or negatives over and over with conviction you either are letting go of or holding on to.

Are you letting go or holding on today with conviction?

How are your problems making you feel?

In your mind are they going from bad to worse?

Are you constantly getting knocked down regardless of what actions you take?

Are you full of despair?

Do you see no way out of your problems?

Love is the ultimate goal to a better understanding of life.

May I be an example of God's strength, hope, joy, freedom, peace, giving, serenity, light, and unconditional love for others to see through my trials, tribulations and experiences......

Fear is a warning that something is not right.

When reflecting on fear it is difficult to accept that I am not in control.

If I surrender to that fear though prayer, meditation, and sharing - my fears lessen.

If I continue to take positive actions the gifts of faith and courage can be received.

With faith and courage as a guide anything is possible!

Even the change on how I react to fear.

There is nothing anyone of us can do that is more important than helping another person.

Anyway we can!

Perseverance will show you a new way to live.

It will make you strong.

Through that strength you will continue to persevere.

If not you will give up and perish.

Then what would the point be?

So it is persevere or perish!

I've learned I can find some peace of mind if I take a few moments of private time.

In that alone time the peace, tranquility, and balance I lost can be restored and that turmoil between my ears, known as my head, is ready to deal with life's challenges once again!

Rationalizations, explanations, excuses, deceit, and alibis are all forms of dishonesty and without honesty there is no spiritual growth.

We were not even aware of how dishonest we were.

We were so self-deceived we believed our own lies.

When we surrendered to the truth God entered and the spiritual process stared.

We no longer were trying to define the truth so we just surrendered to it.

Today we surrender to the truth and we accept the reality that the spiritual process is all about God in our life.

Ever notice a series of events occurring around you that make no sense at all.

Ever notice when you trust that every step you're taking on this path is more valuable than the step before.

Ever notice how fear, anger, disappointed, frustration and pride start dissolving right in front of our eyes.

Isn't it easy for us to forget everything up to this point on this path is a practice for the good things that come our way one step at a time...

Today in spite of any problems, challenges, and circumstances that are bothering you, those things you can or can't see.

These problems, challenges, and circumstances will all be taken care of.

Just as well as everything else today will continue to work out for the very best as they always have.

That is what Faith, Trust, and Love are all about.

The top of the heap or the bottom of the pile

Everyone or no one

Gentle or hard

Hot or cold

Peaks or valleys

Sensitive or aggressive

Love or hate

One extreme or another

Our goal is to find balance……

Sometimes we get there by going to extremes

Other times we seek, learn, strive, and practice

In all cases our goal is balance that precious middle ground with God, others, and self!

Unity happens when I become "part of" rather than "separate from".

This is the place where I get to see how much and where I changed and how much more work there is still to do!

We communicate with others by putting our feelings into words that are kind, considerate, tolerant, giving and loving.

Not by telling them what they should think, feel, or do!

*With God there is no problem or situation
that can shake my peace, freedom, serenity,
and love.*

*Because that's how God's mercy and grace
works no matter what is going on around
me!*

Fear has occupied much of our time and feelings.

These fears generate more negative energy.

God gives us the opportunity to turn our fears and negative energy over to Him.

I will look and see what fears and negative energy I am holding on to in my head and my heart.

I will let go by turning them over to God in prayer and meditation followed with positive action!

*One thing at a time, one second at a time,
one moment at a time, one minute at a time,
one hour at a time, one day at a time......*

Is no waste of time!

Within us is the presence of God.

*Spirituality is the place in which God's
presence shows itself through you to others
by the way of love.*

When I do not engage in selfish and self-seeking motives……

I can give time and energy to rest, prayer, and meditation!

Then I am able to I experience joy, patience, gratitude, understanding, serenity, and love through this process.

Right process and right motives, nice way to live life.

Love is a gift both given and received.

If we had understood this fact maybe we would not have struggled with so much isolation, alienation, and pain.

Our relationship today with God, others, and self provide us with direction, substance, and love that we give and receive.

When we rush, rush, rush and hurry, hurry, hurry we create frustration, anxiety, tension, and impatience, for ourselves.

If we slow down and let things happen by going with the flow we accomplish more by doing less.

Hence "Easy does it"……

Today I pray:

God help me to do my share in making the world a better place by being part of the solution and not part of the problem.

Spirituality means many things to many people.

To me it means seeing oneself as they really are with a sincere attempt to become a better person.

Of course, there will still be many challenges for this is part of life.

These challenges will serve to make you a better person in everything you encounter on this journey.

When I feel alone, blocked, lost, and unable to move I am not!

When I ask for help then help will come.

God sends that help in the way of Angels, Eskimos, and Indians put on my path to show me the way.

Today I will find God among the Angels, Eskimos, and Indians put on my path......

On this journey called life having goals, setting priorities, and taking actions will move us forward......

Fooling ourselves comes with the fact that we are lying, deceiving, manipulating, resentful, controlling, and fearful.

Our ability to stop fooling ourselves comes from the awareness of honesty: with self, others, and God!

Our actions speak volumes louder than anything we say.

We may never know this truth because we are too busy speaking and not taking action.

So show me don't tell me I hear much better that way!

When I am absorbed in self I am unable to overcome the obstacles that block me from God.

I lose the ability to see things clearly.

When I take time in prayer and meditation with God, I gain a new clarity, ability, and vision to overcome the obstacles that were blocking me!

I am then able to receive and accept His love and grace.

I was self- centered - I was selfish - I was angry - I was wrong - I was full of fear - I was resentful - I was lost - I was hanging on to old ideas and beliefs.

No wonder I could find no personal healing.

Then slowly I began to see that the way I was living had to change.

But how do I surrender self and find that healing?

That's what the spiritual journey is all about!

Do you think the reason people do not meditate on a regular basis is because they think it's too hard?

Maybe they do not see that meditation has to be practiced with vigilance and discipline the same way your early prayer life was.

Here is another spiritual tool for growth if you use it!

Keep me mindful of my attitudes and actions.

Keep me going on the right path and direction.

Keep a watchful eye over me.

This I pray.

Reflecting, pondering and dwelling on God are forms of prayers and also ways of meditating......

A prayer for others:

May you be gentle to yourself......

May your thoughts be filled with happiness and love......

May the world be kind to you......

May God keep you in the palm of his hand......

*Have you ever felt all alone with no friends,
laughter, health, or happiness?*

*That place in self where you were stuck, lost,
limited by your circumstances or just unable
to change?*

*Then open your heart and ask God in – take
the actions that would help you to work your
way into better thinking through Gods
guidance!*

Awareness + Forgiveness + Action = Humility

Through action we are capable of achieving many things.

By taking the actions of willingness, honesty, open-mindedness, caring, giving and loving others we receive a new Power in our lives.

Through that Power we gained a new freedom.

Through that freedom and Power we now have a choice in determining the direction in which our lives are heading.

Although nothing much happened until we practiced actions, prayer and meditation to let that Power in.

When I leaned upon money, property, prestige, people, and other things I was never satisfied.

I was always trying to fill that emptiness with outside stuff.

Now that I lean upon you God I am never disappointed.

I do not need to believe in the way others say I must believe for you to be in my life.

You have shown me your presence over and over again.

You have never asked or told me how to believe.

Nor have you pushed me on others to tell them this is how they must believe.

You are all powerful, all encompassing, and all inclusive never exclusive.

You are spiritual not religious.

That's because you are God and not man!

Today and everyday is God's day.

I am thankful for all the blessings of this day.

God's love is in all things in my life.

Today is a day of gratitude for all God's gifts.

I learned what it is to be human.

I am not perfect.

I try to improve my behavior.

I accept my responsibilities.

I aspire to be the best that I can be.

I am not God.

Life's happenings are one thing after another.

Some easy, some hard, some joyous, some sad, some calming, some frustrating, some problem free, some problem filled and they all need time, attention, consideration, and action.

We always have some sorts of: conflicts, challenges, stress, delays, interruptions, disappointments, experiences, changes, and lessons going on that can overwhelm us.

They can stifle us or elate us.

In all these times if we can remember to pause, ask God in, be grateful, let go of managing, control, and outcomes then we can accomplish more by doing less.

Miraculously life's happenings now become one blessing after another no matter what we see, feel, or think.

It's all good no it's all God!

Inappropriate actions will always be inappropriate!

My actions speak volumes louder than any words I say.

May I remember to ask God in to help me?

May I reflect on what actions I'm about to take and what I'm going to do before I do it!

May I always thank God!

My life is filled with all kinds of stuff like: responsibilities, expectations, frustrations, demands, anger, and all sorts of other things.

When I get caught up in them I lose my sight and purpose.

When I take the time to slow down, breath, take it easy, and not get excited then I get an opportunity to see things more clearly.

When I focus on the spiritual rather than the material my life makes sense for everything that surrounds me is covered in love.

When I am able to extend that love to all that is around me I continue to grow and become more spiritually centered.

To pray, pause and be still……

That is how I get fulfilled by You!

Do something for someone today.

More importantly don't let them or anyone else know you did it.

Anonymity at its best!

When I do not know which way to turn lead me.

When I resist prod me.

When I am in pain soothe me.

When I am broken heal me.

When I am lost show me.

When I am hurtful forgive me.

And God always fill me with Your love.

This I pray......

There is no lie or deception that can be hidden or concealed that will not eventually come to light of day for all to see.

That's a good reason to practice honesty!

Fear twists our perceptions, desires, wants, needs, and beliefs of how we see ourselves and others.

It's an illusion, delusion, and lie that will and often does paralyze us from taking action because of our justification, rationalization, and procrastination.

With prayer, meditation, guidance, and the examples of others we see more clearly of how our twisted thoughts kept us a prisoner of self and incapable of taking action.

Action is the solution to remove fear and release us from the prison of self!

Anger, fear, resentment and the like these are the destructive powers which block us from the Sunlight of the Spirit.

How can I rid myself of theses excesses of negative emotions?

First - pray that my heart be cleansed of wrong thinking and wrong actions.

Next – be completely forthright with God, myself, and another human begin.

With this approach – the actions I take are honorable and humble and my character will be taken care of……

AMAZING GRACE at work!

Happiness is the byproduct from positive actions, attitudes, disciplines, and responsibilities to God, self, and others.

Through surrender I became more comfortable with myself, God, and others.

Through acceptance my relationships changed as I became happier and freer.

Through experiences I've learned to enjoy the journey no matter what is on the path.

Speak from your heart and not your head for this is where the real you lives.

You will never know the amounts of joy, happiness, and love that you gave to others already.

That's what makes you special.

Trust in God because He can

Belief in God because He will

Faith in God because He does

This is our greatest success in life!

By practicing prayer and meditation we learn to relax, take it easy, be at peace, and not struggle.

There will come a time when we will understand what eludes us now.

That awareness and understanding comes from God.

It happens in God's time not ours.

So keep practicing!

When we spend time alone with God and seek His guidance He prepares us to better give to others.

That time alone will also ready us to receive and accept what others give to us.

God's messages and gifts comes in the alone with Him and the giving and receiving with each other!

When a heart is filled with gratitude, giving, joy, consideration, thankfulness, goodness, blessings and love it cannot be caught up in life's negativities!

With spiritual principles as a guide like: trust, prayer, faith, meditation, action, selflessness, love, and God, the selfish self-centered experiences, concepts, and ideas I held on to, began to change.

Living each day by spiritual principles, not by the old self-centered and selfish ones I had.

I now can appreciate life and live it to the fullest.

Once I able to expose my hidden faults, defects, and sins by placing them on paper I am then able to take them from the darkness and bring them into a new light.

Once I discuss them with another those faults, defects, and sins lose their power for God is cleansing and healing my heart.

*Am I trying to manage and control –
Powerlessness*

Am I fretting or worrying over it - Prayer

Is it mine or is it someone else's – Inventory

*Seeing this I can practice: If it's mine I apply
and if it's not mine I let it fly!*

Whenever we are whirling and spinning we can take a moment to ask God in, slow down, pray and meditate.

When we do we stop whirling and spinning and we find calm.

So that is how we start our day over!

When our perspectives are based in feelings, thoughts, fears, and motives we are self-centered.

When our perspectives are based in kindness, understanding, consideration, and love we are God centered.

Is my perspective self-centered or God centered?

My attitude affects my life, experiences, thoughts, actions, relationships, and outcomes both positive and negative.

I can embrace this day with a positive attitude or I can embrace this day with a negative attitude.

My attitude is always dependent on whether I'm God centered or self-centered.

The true identity of a person is determined by their physical, mental, emotional, and spiritual capacities for growth, development, acceptance, and change.

Let me not forget that laughter is one of the most precious gifts in life I've been given!

Anger, pride, worry, and fear block God's love and light in our hearts.

Through awareness, surrender, examination, and contemplation we become free to express God's love and light from our hearts as the blocks are removed.

Getting what we want no matter what, is not usually the best course for us to take.

At some point in our life it comes to motives.

Is it selfish, self-centered or is it loving, God centered?

When it's selfish, self-centered it's a bad motive.

When it's loving, God centered it's a good motive.

Simple!

Life is not about what you do or don't do.

What you have or don't have.

What you are or are not.

That would be judgmental, selfish and self-centered.

Life is about being nonjudgmental, selfless, giving, and unconditionally loving.

In other words life is all about God!

Is there a resentment you are holding on to?

Is there a grudge you won't let go?

Is there something you still regret?

You can hang on to it a little longer......

Or you can practice prayer and forgiveness and let it go!

What is your choice?

We all need help in improving and changing our lives.

Some of that help can be seen and there is much help that comes from the unseen and unknown.

We may have much evidence and maybe even some trust in what is seen.

But it takes a great amount of courage as well as an act of faith and belief to venture into the unknown and unseen.

It was in the unseen and unknown that we relied on God and were given the gifts of faith, strength, courage, belief, trust, help, and vision to improve and change our lives.

It was only our fear and pride that kept us from the help we needed!

When we see the world the way we want it to be rather than the way it really is we are self-deceived.

That self-deception is a lie.

Lying is stealing from ourselves and others not just by what we say but by what we do.

All lies are self inflicted.

All lies shut us out from others.

All lies keep us in fear, isolation, loneliness, and despair.

All lies keep us a prisoner, lost and not living in the real world.

The truth sets us free!

When we spend time in prayer and meditation we can relax.

We can enjoy what we are doing savoring the moment.

We can see a glimpse of God's timelessness, peace, quiet, consciousness, trust, patience, acceptance, eternity, and love.

We can slow down and enjoy the presence and fullness of God.

So why don't we spend more time in prayer and meditation?

When we are grateful for life and God in and all around us.

Then we are more aware of the peace, joy and love, which surround us.

Our spirit is uplifted.

We go about our day feeling lightness, peace, joy ease, and love for we were touched by Gods presence.

There is no way for us to reach God from the outside it has to come from within......

Many times in life changing transformation happens quickly.

More often life changing transformation usually comes more slowly.

Either way life changing transformation shows up exactly when it is supposed to!

Facing life's challenges helps us to grow in effectiveness, strength, and responsibility.

Surrendering to life's challenges draws us closer to God.

Accepting God gets us through no matter what life's challenges or conditions can do!

With God as our guide in all our decisions we come to believe that all we experience are expressions of God!

This brings us relief in our times of struggle.

Since perfection is nonexistent for humans the best we will ever be is perfectly imperfect......

In meditation pay no attention to the wandering of the mind.

Instead gently bring your thoughts or attention back and begin again, and again.

Center and re-center self until eventually over time with practice,

perseverance, discipline, and vigilance the mind stops wandering.

Or just pay attention to wandering of the mind.

Either way it is meditation.

We just need to do it regularly to get the much desired results and benefits!

The more you learn to lean on God - the stronger you become.

The stronger you become - the more you learn to lean on God.

I thought God entered my heart in prayer, meditation, silence, guidance, nature, beauty, people, life and love.

So I keep trying to put God into my heart by these things and by what I do.

I finally realized God is not trying to enter my heart He was trying to break out of it.

When I freed God, God freed me!

We cannot grow spiritually while holding onto negativity.

If our negativity festers it will eventually consume us with anger, hate, fear and resentment.

We cannot stop our negativity by simply deciding so.

When our pain gets great enough we make a willing surrender to let go of the negativity that is blocking us.

Through positive action our negativity lessens and we again grow spiritually.

"Simple but not easy"......

If you are struggling, confused, resentful, or afraid ask yourself:

Where is God in all this?....

The more I focused on my negative feelings the more I became an expert on putting myself down.

With these negative feelings and attitudes all I saw were problems.

I did not believe I was capable of any goodness, happiness or love.

How can I change these feelings, attitudes, problems, and negativity?

By asking God and others for help and then taking the actions I learned on my journey.

I am becoming a better person than I ever believed was possible.

Today I know I have a capacity for goodness, happiness, and love no matter what is going on in my life!

Am I spiritual or religious?

Do I see God in my decisions and actions?

Do I see God in the world around me?

Do I see God in what is true and real?

Do I see God in all people?

Spirituality is not about being religious it's about finding and discovering God in me and around me!

Deepen your awareness through prayer and meditation.

Keep an open mind and listen to all that's around you.

In all that you think and do practice peace, joy and love.

Accomplish more by doing less.

You will now have more time and energy as a result of these actions.

Spirituality nurtures peace, happiness, joy, freedom, harmony, and love.

The spiritual healing we experience is God's grace in our lives.

Throughout our life we have to repeatedly adapt to new situations, ideas, and problems.

As our ability to do this grows then a new calm and peaceful demonstration is shown.

Through these actions our life is enriched!

We don't need to do anything to receive God's love.

There is no action we can take to earn God's love.

When we rest and don't struggle God's love comes to us.

Trusting in God's love is all it takes for us.

We know that our life is now in God's hands.

These actions come from God not from us.

Can you see God's grace?

There is an unseen Power in front of me that guides me......

There is an unseen Power behind me that pushes me......

There is an unseen Power within me that fulfills me......

God is that unseen Power that guides, pushes, and fulfills me!

Today I will take the time to seek, find, and feel God's presence within me because I am a child of God worthy of His love and care......

God sets me free to be me!

God's power can accomplish anything.

There is no limit to what God can do.

With God anything is possible and can happen if only we believe.

God is all we need and all that it takes.

What we receive from God is faith, reliance, and trust.

Not bad… if only we believe.

Freedom in mind, body, and spirit means that we are one with God.

God dwells in, around, and through us.

He removes all that blocks his presence keeping us one with Him and free......

We all need forgiveness whether we are giving it to others or we are asking for ourselves.

We seem to be blocked form forgiveness by hurt feelings, bitterness, pride, resentment, anger, and fear.

That battle is what goes on between our head and our heart.

With the help others, prayer, meditation, and guidance from God forgives is possible, attainable, and achievable.

Once the battles and blocks are gone forgives happens!

The more we come to God the more freely and fully God flows into us.

The more open we are to receive the more God gives.

So why do we resist?

The roads and pathways to meet God are many.

Spiritual signs, awakenings, and experiences are all around for us to see and make use of.

God is constantly expressing His presence and spirit in our lives.

When God moves in us and we feel His spirit we suddenly find God everywhere, in everything, even in the smallest of details.

Spiritual signs, awakenings, and experiences are wonderful daily events.

The beauty of the Spiritual roads and pathways that we travel is that they are ours and ours alone.

They are there for us to reach out and meet God......

Every day is filled with God's wonders if we only take the time to look and see!

In life we will always have challenges.

How we meet these challenges will not only determine our character.

It will also determine our ability to prepare, grow, overcome, and move forward in life.

The 12 Step process allowed my head to meet my heart through the Love that I was so freely given.

Finally I was paying attention to the dance my heart was doing with God.

That long journey we take between our head and our heart, that place where Love and God are found.

How often have we procrastinated about our obligations, commitments, and responsibilities?

Procrastination is not about easy or hard, fun or boring, and right or wrong.

Procrastination is all about avoiding obligations, controlling commitments, and managing responsibilities.

When we take actions and not worry about outcomes there is no place for procrastination!

To care, to give, to hope, to love these are the traits we need as we adventure into the unknown and unseen......

The idea that we were responsible for others feelings, happiness, or sadness is a lie we told ourselves.

This faulty destructive belief system caused us guilt and shame.

Were we victims or volunteers?

Were we allowing others to have control over us?

We no longer have to allow these faulty destructive beliefs have control over our feelings or our lives.

God makes that possible.

Through the help of God and others we begin setting ourselves free from any faulty destructive beliefs we have.

Keep knocking on new doors so that change has an opportunity.

The few who adjust to make the progress of change possible will keep moving forward no matter how difficult things may be.

Do not carry these changes in your heart only.

Share your experience of change so others may find hope.

Fear is the only thing that is in the way of me moving forward in life.

When I am harboring resentments against someone and I find it too difficult for me to let go of......

Then I need to pray for that person to receive all the good things I wish for myself.

I am to continue praying for that person until I truly mean it or until God softens and changes my heart.

If we chase our wants we feel secure temporarily.

We will continue to seek happiness, love, and security through someone or something else.

If we seek God our needs will be met and we will become truly happy, genuinely loving, and eternally secure.

Why do we still chase our wants instead seeking God for our needs?

When we chase people and things to fill the emptiness within us we are on the wrong path.

All we need to do is seek a spiritual not a material solution.

To change that path we are on we need help.

We need the help of others and God.

Others help to guide us on this path and the grace of God to fulfill us.

The place we seek that solution is within.

Our path then changes!

We seek God first, then the help of others, and think about ourselves least.

Through that process we find freedom, peace, and happiness.

Not a bad road to travel.

Today:

I know myself

I know how to be honest

I seek to make amends for my wrongs

I am responsible

I am teachable

I live by principles

I enjoy my life

I am not afraid to stand alone for what I believe

I seek to love

I seek God

I seek to serve

I have a lot going on!

When we apply honesty, open-mindedness, and willingness in our lives we find the strength we need to go forward and grow spiritually.

Do you give of yourself before someone even asks?

When you do you enter into realm of the spirit.

This is what living a spiritual life is really all about!

When a man and a woman (significant others) can be interdependent of each other then and only then can they have a healthy relationship!

When we do not force ourselves by making things happen by trying to adjust situations to our liking.

When instead we just let them happen - then life opens up before us.

So simple yet so hard!

Balance is achieved through the nurturing of self mentally, emotionally, physically, and spiritually.

Faith makes the darkest times bearable.

Act as if things have already come to pass.

Know there will always be challenges.

See Faith working as you change your attitudes, insights and perceptions.

With Faith you are going to have a new clarity and a new peace of mind.

It's not always easy to let go or change our feelings of guilt, remorse, and shame.

By dealing with today instead of focusing on our past......

By living today as it comes instead of regretting our past......

By doing what we know is right today everything will take care of itself......

God has forgiven our past mistakes!

So why can't we?

The healing power we receive comes from trusting God, sharing of ourselves, and helping others.

Through taking these actions we receive the gifts of; courage, strength, change, and harmony with God......

When we run into difficulties that seem impossible to overcome we can always look back to see what made it possible to overcome them......

Change requires: risk, courage, giving up, pain, trying, willingness, selflessness, vulnerability, responsibility, consequences, readiness, acceptance, failing, success, pleasure, rejection, want, desire, focus, action, practice, and surrender.

Without a degree of these qualities nothing changes.

And if nothing chances I stagnate and die a spiritual death.

A price I'm not willing to pay anymore.

So change I must and change I do!

God moves in me, around me, and through me with every breath I take.

God fills my mind and body with His light and love.

Every cell of my body responds to God's love for me.

I am assured that in accordance with God's perfect design all will be well.

For that I am eternally grateful.

Distorted perceptions, attitudes, behaviors, thoughts, and actions are a direct result of my negativity!

With each ending there is a new beginning, path, or journey for us to follow.

Each new beginning, path, or journey is designed for one purpose.

That purpose is to bring us closer to God!

Have you ever seen something, read something, or heard something and the message just hit you right in the heart?

That feeling you got just may be God presence waking you up!

God is the sustaining and maintaining Presence in all things.

You don't have to go anywhere to find God.

God is already there.

Therefore relax in the realization that God is the only Presence and Power we need.

Because God is - we do not need any other powers......

*When I walk hand and hand with the
limitations of self I'm lost in darkness.*

*Prayer will break through the limitations of
self and darkness and shine God's light on
my human weakness.*

*God will remove my darkness, limitations,
and weaknesses when I seek and do His will
and not mine!*

Life means responding not reacting.

Life means not avoiding fear, problems, situations, pitfalls, and negativities.

Life means joy, happiness and freedom.

Life means experience.

Life means living.

Are we here to be tested, suffer, or judged?

Are we here to make things happen?

Are we here to put the needs of others first?

Are we here to learn tolerance or acceptance?

Are we here to find a purpose?

I truly believe God has us here to spread His LOVE.

What do you believe?

There comes a time to re-examine our lives and our values.

It is at this point, we discover what is really important.

We rid ourselves of playing the victim or the martyr.

We hesitate less in asking for help.

We finally take responsibility for ourselves and all our actions.

We now can move forward and finally have a strong interpersonal relationship with God, ourselves, and others.

The choices and decisions I make directly influence the quality of my life.

There is no longer the blaming of others for decisions, attitudes, actions, and choices that were made.

Today I accept full responsibility and accountability for all decisions, attitudes, actions, and choices that are and were made.

I no longer feel helpless and powerless over the events of my life.

Today the quality of my life has changed I've gained a sense of well-being, peace, and love that is absolutely miraculous.

People, places, and things in our life create experiences for us.

These experiences create memories.

Experiences and memories help us know what to hold on to and what to let go of.

Through this process our personal growth and understanding continues unfolding.

With this awareness our life starts creating new experiences and new memories through people, places, and things.

Over and over and over!

When we belittle our feelings, opinions, achievements, and needs we can't do anything and believe were helpless.

Then we find ways to destroy whatever we are doing so we believe we are worthless.

With helplessness and worthlessness as our guide we fall into self pity.

When we stop giving into the lie that we are helpless, worthless, and full of self pity then we see the truth and gain a new strength, attitude, and direction.

The strength of God!

The attitude of hope!

The direction of faith, trust, and new beliefs!

We now become helpful, worthy, giving and loving.

We listen, we hear, we share, we trust, we sense, we choose, we encourage, we support, we try, we help, we care, we experience, we like, we want, we ask, we agree, we disagree, we process, we continue, we suggest, we think, we have, and we love!

Sounds like a good foundation for a healthy relationship.

It does not matter how bad the past has been!

As we accept the past our perceptions change.

When we let go of the past we begin a new future.

Each and every day we gain new hope.

When we run on self will the little things become big things and the big things become even bigger.

We become unable to understand or solve our difficulties.

Everything becomes too much for us.

We become confused and lost.

We need God's help.

When we seek God's help our problems seem to solve themselves.

Everything becomes clearer.

And our will is suddenly lining up with Gods!

Sometimes we feel we did not do our best.

We were not paying attention to anyone but ourselves.

Our own actions and attitudes kept us blocked from God.

When we surrendered we were no longer blocked.

Our actions and attitudes became God centered not self centered!

When we approach situations in our lives with gratitude we experience a sense of well-being.

That well-being brings us happiness and joy.

The end result of that happiness and joy is change.

That change comes because of the way we approach life situations and events with gratitude.

Through my thoughts and actions today I will perceive nothing but good things coming to me.

I will work toward that end and leave the results to God.

So that's what is meant by 10% Inspiration and 90% Perspiration!

There's nothing absolutely nothing that a grateful heart and soul can't overcome, become, do, or have!

In time eventually......

God did not do what I wanted Him to do when I wanted Him to do it.

So I was angry at God.

Not doing what I wanted when I wanted was God's answer.

I know today God says yes, no, and wait.

He usually says wait before yes or no so I can practice not being angry!

Keep me aware as I go through my day that there is nothing in this world that cannot be overcome with God's help!

Do you think that happiness is having all you want?

No it's not having all you want and knowing that you don't have to have it!

The experience of patience comes when I'm in touch with gratitude.

What I am expecting and accepting from others may I expect and accept from myself......

Love is not easy.

Love is not just about caring, feeling, attraction, and commitment.

Love is all about our actions of selfless giving.

Simple just not easy......

Everything that is happening right now needs to happen. Stay focused on the present; ask God for help, take action, trust in the process, and the future will take care of itself.

By applying Spiritual values in your life you will uncover a greater awareness and an appreciation for all that surrounds you.

Do not respond to a busy mind when it's filled with anger, doubt, expectations, negativity, and fear.

Instead quiet that busy mind through prayer, meditation, and love.

Then you can respond with a thankful heart and mind.

Have you ever wondered whether or not you would make it through those dark tough times?

Or that that life was supposed to be easy, fair or just?

As time passed were you surprised by how well it was all working out?

Did you reflect on the courage, discipline, hard work of the actions you were taking?

What did you tell yourself then?

Did you see how Gods Love lead you to discovery a new attitude, excitement, freedom, and peace through those dark tough times?

All of it has nothing to do with how much or what you or you did, are doing, or going to do!

The Gift of God's Grace – WOW

The people who reach out to help others never run out of things to do.

They often don't know what they can do until it is already done; what they can become until they already arrived there; or what can happen until it's already past.

The difference we make in other people's lives to us is always less than the difference other people make in our lives.

We all have problems, fears, and worries.

When we spend time and energy controlling our feelings and situations our negativities keep increasing.

We become emotionally absent.

Even when everything is going well we feel insecure.

We feel something is not right.

We turn our fears and insecurities over to God.

When we do this we were no longer caught up in self.

We finally are able to live free from our self made prisons!

Persistence - is about knocking on one door, then another, and another until all possible doors are knocked on and one finally opens!

My thoughts, feelings, inspirations, are all seeds planted by God to grow me into the person he wants me to be......

God I pray that you will guide me, help me, direct me, show me, and love me today and every day.

I know you will do all this when I surrender and give my will and my life to your care.

I surrender - please take all of me God - direct my ways - so I may I grow, feel, reflect on your presence, and love today and always......

By starting and ending our day with spiritual readings, prayer, meditation, and guidance we are seeking and thanking God.

At first we do this whether we feel like it or not.

With time our spiritual journey changes.

Our spiritual readings, prayer, meditation, and guidance become second nature to us and suddenly whether we know it or not the unexpected happens.

We are now doing this because we want to know God better.

Miracles do happen!

Spiritual surrender is not letting go of your external material possessions.

It is the opening of your heart to spiritual internal principles and well being that only comes from your soul.

Spiritual surrender is giving your-self to God.

The battle that never ends!

Prayer, encouragement, charity, a smile, or a kind word, are all opportunities to get out of self and give to others.

The question is how, when, what, and where, to give?

Are these the real questions and opportunities or is God really drawing us closer to Him!

When what I think and do about you is more important than what I think and do about me...... That's codependency

When what I think and do about me is more important than what I think and do about you...... That's selfish and self-centeredness

When what I think and do about you is equally important to what I think and do about me...... That's balance and interdependency and this is truly what sets us free!

"God is the light, the truth, and the way"

The light is Awareness.

The truth is Love.

The way is Action.

It's all God!

Prayer was the beginning of a spiritual life.

Then there was spiritual readings and literature to feed, open, and fire the mind.

Then there was sharing and guidance with others to show us a path to continue on our spiritual growth.

Then we begin to start the day and turn within in meditation and the search for the ultimate infinite truth spiritually.

Then God revealed Himself and we are fed from within.

Then we found God Consciousness.

Then the spirit of God that lives within started flowing, teaching, strengthening and inspiring our spiritual journey.

Each of these is only a part of our spiritual tapestry and journey.

"More will be revealed"

I have failed in my life in so many ways but somehow I never failed altogether.

You were working with me even when I thought you deserted me.

You are my strength and my sustenance in all times regardless of what I feel, think, want, do, or what is going on.

God I thank you for the gifts and grace even when I'm not aware they are there!

Be the love you want the world to see!

Time with God daily transforms us mentally and spiritually.

I do not understand these transformations because they are beyond my knowledge and understanding.

All I know is that these transforming experiences keeps happening since spending daily time with God......

ONE PROCESS OF SURRENDER TO CHANGE

1. *Awareness*
2. *Admittance*
3. *Acceptance – with or without approval*
4. *Surrender – as much as we can at this moment*
5. *Change*

Over and Over

May I see and learn the principles of living the good life.

May I pray and meditate upon them.

May I work at them because they are Gods will for me!

Prayer and meditation is the way to link and improve our personal and spiritual relationship with God!

There are many rewards for those who follow a spirit filled life as well as many obstacles on the path.

Both are gifts from God!

On your spiritual journey have you gone farther than you could have ever imagined or dreamed?

We seem to focus on memories whether fancied or real that were bad for us.

We have a way to assist our memory by the process of taking inventory then sharing it with another and God.

We gain the ability to see those defects that block and/or disturb us.

We can ask God for their removal.

We have gratitude for all the good and bad that comes our way and helps us keep our balance as we see things more clearly.

We are then able to receive God's grace from this process.

The reason I enjoy my solitude and alone time is because I never am anymore.

Through the spiritual journey I have been blessed with many tools and gifts on my path.

God help me to remember to use these tools and gifts on a daily basis.

When I do it brings me closer to you!

Finding answers to any problem that we encounter means finding someone who has had experience with the same types of situations or problems.

Once we find that person we open up about what is going on.

It's unreal how they hear us with an understanding, compassion, patience, and empathy we never thought possible.

We then realize we are no longer alone and we become willing to take the necessary actions to overcome whatever is blocking us.

Through this process we find a new freedom, joy, happiness, and serenity.

Amazing how this works!

In prayer ask God to use you as a vehicle and to guide you.

The words and actions come as you become one of God's vehicles to help others.

Everything will work for the best even though it may not seem that way.

There are always reasons to be happy if you only stop and honestly look.

People think of you and call you their friend.

Lives are touched by your presence.

With this kind of gratitude in your heart it is impossible to fail.

Your spirit lives and things just keep getting better.

God's Love

You can never be outside the realm of God's love, ever flowing, ever giving, and ever permeating you. If you are struggling with something in life today, take a time out, relax, and listen in the silence.

There is no problem, no situation, no hurt, and nothing that God cannot heal. God's love is always giving life and life is never ending. Life flows through you and not at you through God's love.

The healing you receive may not be the way you think it should be. Yet it is always being done with the Power of God's Love.

We base decisions on the best information we have in front of us right now......

We can always reevaluate our decisions with new information, facts, and circumstances as they are revealed.

Then we get to make new decisions.

Over and over again and again!

Be careful of what you pray for because you might just get it.

Getting it might not be good for you.

Then you will be praying to have it removed.

Once again you are praying for your will not God's.

It is better to pray only for God's will no matter what that is.

It always works out better that way!

Controlling others' behaviors cannot be done.

We don't have the power to make anybody think, feel, or do anything.

We can only show by our encouragement, behaviors, and experiences the love we received and how we changed.

We do this by getting out of the way and letting God shine through and not telling others what to do!

When you speak of the past, present, and future: speak of the past gratefully, speak of the present enthusiastically, and speak of the future hopefully!

When we take responsibility for our behaviors and actions we are seeking to live and grow closer to our fellows and God!

Forgiveness sets the prisoner free......

And that prisoner was always me!

If you change direction you are headed down a different path at least that's what it looks like to you.

Did you ever think, see, and believe you may not end up where you thought you were heading?

Do not be discouraged it just might be God's way of taking you where He wants you to be!

Many times in life we believe there is no way out.

We are filled with doubt, confusion, and fear.

It is only by embracing God that it becomes clear.

God is only drawing us near.

Suddenly no more doubt, confusion, and fear!

What everybody else knows about us is not as important as what God knows about us and what we know about us is least important!

I seek God by the longing in my heart to be near and loved by Him.

Spiritual values are the greatest gift we have to share with others......

May we never forget; one small act of kindness can have a life changing effect and impact on another that we may never know we had anything to with......

There are times we feel, think, and believe we are alone.

These moments are designed for us to stop, reflect, search, find, and reconnect to our spiritual self.

Once this is done we can step out with faith and courage and move on!

It matters not what name we call it by.

We are all here on the path to unite in oneness with it.

The path to truly connect with our purpose for being here!

Thanks to God I have been granted the ability to stay calm, centered, and at peace, regardless of all that surrounds me.

And for that I am eternally grateful......

Fear is often accompanied with loneliness.

We don't have to face anything alone or in isolation.

All we have to do is ask for help.

Once we do we are nurtured, guided, protected, and loved right where we are in spite of our isolation, feelings, failings, loneliness, thoughts, or fears.

So why do we struggle so much when it comes to asking for help?

As we are spiritually fed our minds and souls are nourished with inner peace and tranquility as God's presence fills us.

It is with these experiences and spiritual feedings that we have the ability to be grounded.

So it is when we come into contact with individuals who are spiritually centered or when we have spiritual feedings that a new understanding of God comes into view.

With this presence of God the dark disappears as the light shines through.

As we accept being spiritually fed the mind, body, and spirit are awakened by God's presence and power.

When this is brought to our consciousness we understand that we are speaking of God who is individual, personal and intimate.

Believe, learn, trust, listen, and persist in all things spiritual and God will reveal Himself!

If we are insecure, we become restrictive, controlling, and possessive.

We must be free of our insecurities and self centered fears.

By learning to give and not get without any expectations takes time and practice.

As we become less restrictive, controlling, possessive, insecure, and self centered we will become more open, trusting, giving, and loving.

We come to understand that all our relationships are based in love and not fear.

Love freely given is unconditional.

By giving we actually get!

Things seldom happen when we ask for them.

They usually come from someone or something we didn't even know when we first asked.

The results seem to come from some turn of events that was impossible to see when we first started.

That's Gods way of showing His anonymity working in our life!

When we are wondering, controlling, planning, manipulating, figuring out, and worrying what is going to happen next, a little later, tomorrow, this week, next week, later on this month, next month, later this year, next year, on and on……

We are setting ourselves up for disappointments and disappointments are expectations that come to pass!

I see everything through my narrow, limited, selfish views and perspectives.

God sees everything with unconditional love, understanding, and care from its manifestation through its perfect completion.

I pray I may see things more like God and less like me!

We can use words that hurt, control, manipulate and deceive others.

Or we can use words to sooth, give, and love others.

The words we choose can have a powerful and lasting effect......

What words are we choosing?

Awareness is the breakthrough that frees us from self......

We may not succeed but that does not mean we are a failure.

No matter how many times we do not succeed, fall down, are held back, are stifled, or just plain failed, we are not failures.

Until we to blame others!

When we focus on solutions and not on our problems we learn how to change our perceptions, attitudes, and actions.

It's all dependent on whether we focus on perceptions, attitudes, and actions in solutions or in problems.

That's our choice!

God is an individualized and internal expression.

Any way we try to communicate that to others God is lost in the translation.

We all posses many gifts and talents

We all do different kinds of service

We all do our works uniquely

All these individual gifts, talents, service, works, and uniqueness have come from God!

To change the way we perceive and deceive ourselves and others takes time.

We can do this by evaluating our actions, behaviors and habits.

This is way we learn how our negatively affected all our relationships.

Now we want to change and we do change!

When we share our fears and God's answers we light the darkened paths and lift the broken spirits of others!

Inventory taking is a gift that helps us in many ways.

We can see what we want and what we don't want.

We can see what to do and what not to do.

We can see what is real or what is imagined.

We can list what to change and what not to change.

We can focus on ourselves or on others.

We can be present or be aloof.

We can utilize or we can analyze.

Inventory taking helps us end the past and begin the new.

Remember "Yesterday is history – tomorrow is a mystery - today is the present" and that gift comes by taking inventory!

Today I will great solitude with warmth and a smile just as I great an old friend.

With that greeting I will rest in that quite place and time where I can be serine, contemplative and available to God.

In that availability with God I find comfort, deep calmness, inner peace and love.

Today I will seek to experience inner peace and inner calmness through solitude with God.

Setting aside time each day for prayer and meditation is the key to my relationship with God.

When I become hurried, confused, distracted, or lost in this process it does not matter.

In time, the fact is this discipline enhances my relationship with God.

-SIMPLE-

Has the feelings of worthlessness, hatred, chaos, loneliness, self pity, and fear over taken you?

Through friends, action, and love - the hope you once had that seemed to vanish - emerges and a new faith comes into view.

These are the times to see the spiritual opportunities for growth that are present in your life.

It's not what's happening around you that will determine this. It's what's happening inside of you!

Starting to do something today at wherever you are - is the best way to get something accomplished.

If you're not forcing things and are taking affirmative action - you will begin to realize you are creating a new pathway.

That pathway can lead straight to your dreams, miracles or even straight to God.

When I set my busy thoughts aside and seek
God I am able reach a new awareness.

Then moment by moment the tensions,
anxieties, doubts, and fears melt away.

Feelings of calm and comfort fill me.

So why do I hold on to my busy thoughts
instead of seeking God?

Today I will take some time to close my eyes, breathe deeply, relax, and listen to all that surrounds me allowing Gods love to sooth my spirit and fill me.

Through the practice of truth and the power of prayer we are lead to the awareness of faith, wisdom and God's presence in our life.

Why do we question love?

Love is unconditional and not questioning.

Just like God.

In that case why do we question God?

If you are really honest with yourself - you have to admit that things in your life today are far more different than you ever thought they would be.

The only thing that really changes your thinking, feelings, or circumstances is your actions.

You don't need the help of other people with that......

Or do you?

You have a better effect on others when you reach out with understanding, compassion, guidance, comfort, and love.

Just the same way others reached out to you!

When I am full of fear or caught in self may I be reminded that all things are possible when - I ask for help, let go of all my concerns, take appropriate actions, help others, and trust in God.

Why isn't God the first thing?

Oh yea it's all that fear and self stuff in the way!

When I give unconditionally and I freely love - everything else falls into place......

All things are possible when you invite God in and take appropriate action!

We need each other's help to deal with fear for we are all pretty much the same inside.

I must begin to recognize my fears and then I need to take some risk by letting others in to help.

When I accept their help I receive their love.

The lesson to be learned from this is......

Love is the best antidote for fear!

I do not have the ability to turn things around by myself.

I need the help of others and God.

Through others experiences, setbacks, qualities, and guidance I am able to ask God in.

Through practice, action, and discipline God through others shows me the way to turn things around.

I can see how my negative behaviors created the negative feelings I had about myself.

That was the lie I always deceived myself with!

I now see that by taking positive actions on that negativity the way I behave and feel has changed.

That change is I am now able to let go of the lie and see the truth about myself!

I do not always remember to ask God into my life.

When I am distracted I forget to place God first.

When that happens I take Him for granted and forget God is instead of I am.

God is never separated from me although I constantly separate myself from Him.

I always can reconnect to God in prayer and meditation.

God's love is always available unconditionally to me if I only ask!

The opportunities to express gratitude arise from failures turned into assets by God.

By seeking God we are given the strength to rise above failure and express our gratitude.

If we stuff our fears and don't take action our fears continue to grow larger until they paralyze and overtake our lives.

When we write our fears on paper they lose power over us for we see them in a different light.

When we discuss them with another person it will help us not isolate and keep our fears in their proper perspective.

We ask God in to help with our fears.

The actions of: Writing – Discussing - Praying

What a great antidote for fear......

When I ask God to come into my life it is because of a longing in my heart.

If I surrender to that gentle voice within - God's spirit enters my heart.

His peace, grace, and love fill me.

I am then no longer longing.

For my heart is full.

What do we have to share with others?

We share respect, caring, understanding, empathy, money, sympathy, generosity, shelter, food, trust, joy, happiness, humor, experience, strength, hope, love ad infinitum......

We also share about our loneliness, illness, pains, losses, and suffering that we overcame and the blessings we received along the way.

Most importantly we share our God.

Not a bad road or journey to take considering we were mentally, physically, emotionally, and spiritually bankrupt with nothing to share when we arrived!

My life was filled with adversities, struggles, rebounds, comebacks, and triumphs.

All of them were not controlled by me although you could not convince me of that then.

Today I know I have nothing to do with the outcome of what goes on in my life just what actions I take.

The results are up to God!

Surrender happens when give up all that you are unwilling to live without!

It is so easy to blame others for the way we feel.

If others would only behave the way we plan then all would be well.

At least that is what we think because of our selfish self-centered perspective.

It would help us if we open our hearts and minds to a new perspective.

One based in selflessness, understanding, and compassion for another.

Using the principle of giving rather than getting!

When we are able to do that we stop blaming others for the way we feel.

We are no longer dependent on them for our feelings or our happiness.

We are free from the bondage of self.

Pride and fear always put us on the defensive.

Pride and fear will keep us separated from God and our fellows.

Awareness, action, and acceptance of self lead us away from pride and fear and to the reuniting with God and our fellows!

Each day all around us there is much positive and much negative.

We can choose to focus on either one.

What do you chose to focus on today?

Everything in life is in a state of constant change.

The ups and downs we go through are just part of that change.

The ups and downs will come and go.

They visit us to help condition us.

If they didn't visit us everything would be flat and boring.

And we would never have any of the awareness, growth, opportunity, or ability to change!

We all struggle with some sort of pain.

Sometimes the pain seems to be endless.

Sometimes we hang on to the pain out of comfort or fear.

Either way pain then has control of us.

When we surrender our pain to God it loses its control.

If we take the time to reflect on the past pains that we have overcome with God's help, it is easier to change our perspective.

Through this new awareness and perspective from our experiences we now are able to help others with their pain!

Many of us believed we could not get away from ourselves or our old behaviors.

We needed help in straightening out our lives.

We saw examples of others who straightened their lives out.

We did not think it would work for us.

How were we going to become who we wanted to be?

Through surrender, work, and grace a miracle happened.

Our lives straightened out and we became an example for others.

God help me.

God make me aware of your presence in my life today.

God lead me where you want me to be today.

God let me share your goodness with everyone I meet today.

God thank you.

*When we treat others with kindness,
consideration, and love, we will experience
the same in return.*

What we give out is what we will get back!

It is said the solution to any problem lies within.

Every problem can be solved.

When we listen with God to the words of others, pray, meditate, and seek guidance solutions reveal themselves.

We need to be open to it.

The problem was never the problem; the problem was our attitude to the problem.

The solution was always God, prayer, meditation, seeking, guidance, and love!

God inspires us to have the faith to tackle the unknown and unseen.

Inspiration can be given away or received by examples.

Through our example we inspire others.

At other times others inspire us.

It is not us or others that is really doing the inspiring.

It never was.

It was always the unknown and unseen hand and faith of God!

We were lonely.

We were lost.

We couldn't be trusted.

We were angry.

We hurt others.

We hurt ourselves.

*We were mentally, physically, and spiritually
bankrupted.*

*We finally found this place inside of us
where our God lives.*

*We surrendered our will and our lives over to
Him.*

*We were no longer mentally, physically, and
spiritually bankrupted.*

*We found our spiritual center, freedom,
peace, balance, and love in God!*

*Loneliness, suspicion, uncomfortably,
tension, expectations, pain,
disappointments, turmoil, arguments, strife,
denial, indecisiveness, cruelty, pressure,
sarcastic, violent, destructive, stressful,
anger, fear, resentment, etc. etc. etc......*

Love heals them all!

Experiences are a set of guidelines which offers us a way to live.

We learn from each experience a better way of life!

I am perfectly imperfect because God made me that way so my failures and mistakes can help me and others understand, learn, and grow from them.

These human frailties keep me right sized and humble.

They help me to seek God's perfect love more.

We might not always feel or believe God's presence is with us.

This happens when we are playing God and running on self-will.

When we let go, stop struggling, and seek Gods guidance we can sense His presence, tranquility, peace, and love.

Once again we have faith, belief, trust, strength, and knowledge for we know God is with us.

It was our self-centered fear that kept us from Him.

He never left.

All we had to do is "Let Go and Let God".

My instinct is to tell you what you should do.

I had to learn to listen first.

Through this I learned to practice restraint.

Through that restraint I learned to pray.

Through prayer I learned to respond.

By learning to; listen, practice restraint, pray, and respond I am no longer the prisoner of my instinct to tell you what you should do!

Inappropriate language is a lack of respect and consideration for others.

If we show no respect or consideration in our communications with others we are really showing no respect for ourselves.

This behavior is inconsiderate and unacceptable and stops our spiritual growth.

By asking God for help our words and actions change and we grow spiritually.

Experience shows I don't have to always like what is going on in life.

I believe God is taking me to a place where He wants me to be.

I believe God is conditioning me through pain, trust, and love to rely on Him.

When I trust and rely on me, oh well we know what happens, life usually gets worse.

When I trust and rely on God life always works out for the best!

So why do I first trust and rely on me instead of first trusting and relying on God and His love?

My prayers lose their meaning when they become mechanical rhythms and repetition.

Yet there are whole classes of people that pray just that way and that works for them.

So how should I pray?

With prayers that comes through my heart with simplicity so that that my words will continue to take on new meaning, depths, and significance.

I trust that I may find the simplicity I need in prayer by using my heart and not my head!

I continually hold on and cling to many things.

Help me to open my heart and release it all in sweet surrender.

God grant me that kind of willing heart to surrender to Your loving care.

I pray that I may do all I can to love others in spite of mine or their faults.

As I pray God teach me that I love with no expectations of being loved back.

Happiness is a by-product of doing the right thing and living the right kind of a life.

Happiness is God's recognition of our faithfulness to live by spiritual principles.

Happiness is our reward not our destination!

When I feel like I will surely fail and my mind, spirit, and soul is empty.

You bring me new life.

You give me Your love nourishing my mind, spirit, and soul.

I thank You for being on time, every time, all the time even in my darkest moments of doubt!

Many of us think happiness comes from outside of us.

It comes from looking within us not from outside of us.

There is no mystery in finding happiness.

It's when we take responsibility for our own actions and begin to listen to the inner voice of God.

That's when we find happiness.

When we contribute in a loving manner to all the situations and circumstances in and around us then we are doing God's work!

Simple but not easy!

The best way for us to live is by our actions and not our thinking.

It is through our actions we see just how much we really can accomplish.

If we continue to practice living by our actions instead of by our thinking then anything is possible!

Do I avoid the things I do not like? Do I criticize? Do I gossip?

Do I create conflict? Do I consider others inferior to me?

Do I dismiss the thoughts and ideas of others?

Do I judge?

Do I condemn? Do I hide from life?

A new awareness can be gained by questions like these.

Having this awareness without taking the action to change......

Well that's just self deception!

There is always enough time if you first pause, rest, and pray before taking action.

No matter what struggles, challenges, frustrations or fears are in my life today because of negative emotions, behaviors, situations, or actions......

I will continue to seek the Spiritual disciplines which will always lead me on the path I seek to find Gods will and Grace to solve any situation.

Having a meaningful healthy relationship with another human being takes tolerance, nurturing, patience, selflessness, and love.

In other words a meaningful healthy relationship takes work!

Warped, twisted, and defective relationships, acquaintances, and circumstances are very rarely seen for what they are.

These unpleasant problems and negativities are another way for God to enrich our personal and spiritually growth.

Through openness with God, fullness in prayer, meditation, and guidance from others......

We change!

We live life from moment to moment.

Some moments are short, some moments are long, and some moments are even longer.

There are no moments to hard that we can't preserve and stay in them.

As we go through our day we will find no part of it bigger than the moment we are in.

Today I will preserve the best I can by staying in the present moment.

The practice of prayer, meditation, honesty, willingness, courage, open-mindedness, integrity, humility, brotherly love, obedience, discipline, prudence, selflessness, self-sacrifice, inventory-taking and love brings us to a place of spiritual, emotional health, and well being.

All we have to do is practice, practice, practice!

When I was dependent on self I used my knowledge to keep people out, I remained isolated, was full of doubts, mistakes, negativity, and destructive behaviors.

I needed to change.

I wanted to change.

I needed to be shown how to change.

People helped me, showed me, directed me, and loved me so I could discover my journey, growth, and life spiritually.

For that I am eternally grateful!

Lack of love will block Gods light and spirit from entering.

I will seek God's light and spirit where nothing unloving can be.

Many of us have no peace or rest only trials, tribulations, afflictions, and sorrows.

We don't know how we will ever get through them.

We perceive and persevere that our true peace and rest is not in the outward things or stuff.

It lies deep in our hearts with God.

It is only with God that we find true peace of the heart, which no one or nothing can take away from us, and in which there is nothing that cannot be overcome......

How do we change the low self-esteem we have?

We need to look at all the positive possibilities of what will work, rather than focusing on why it won't work.

With the focus on the positive we are able to step out into action.

That action becomes who we are and amazingly our esteem changes for the better.

Our understanding of God is revealed in and through guidance, seeking, spiritual experiences, prayer and meditation.

Constantly!

"It doesn't matter what others do – It only matters what I do!"

Serenity is the place when you are at peace with everything and everyone, no matter how turbulent your journey is or how rough the road.

When opportunities arise that involves acts of kindness - may I always give freely.

Hopefully I will not avoid the opportunity for helping - which Gods places on my path.

God knows I have needed such Love from others in the past!

People who are not spiritually connected do not care about what is going on in your life or what you are really going through.

They are far more interested in what they are going through and it is all about them.

Tell me what self-centered, self-seeking, selfishness and conditional means once again.

By the way where is God in that......

If you're not sure of life's uncertainties or the lack of clarity that is surrounding you be grateful for this awareness.

Once this new awareness is realized give it time.

For only in time will the seeds grow so God can work His miracles.

If you receive criticism from someone don't be angry be grateful for it.

It shows that they care enough to say something that might help you at some level.

With all the struggles in life that we have are we seeking on a daily basis to overcome them by practicing prayer, meditation, and discipline?

Look hard are you diligently participating in your spiritual life?

Isn't that what God intend for us to do?

When we stop dwelling on the wrongs of yesterday we begin enjoying today.

We can only to relive our past wrongs of yesterday by creating a good day, this day, today!

That way tomorrow we can look back without having to dwell on the wrongs of yesterday and say what might have been!

We can set boundaries we need to set.

We can choose a path that works for us.

We can decide what boundaries or decisions are necessary for us.

What is new to us about setting boundaries, choosing paths, or making decisions?

The idea that that we can......

It is better to solve our problems by asking God and others in rather than by pushing and trying to solve them alone.

By stepping back, pausing, and waiting we are given an opportunity through God's help and others guidance to work out our difficulties.

Have I learned to ask in God, relax, take it easy, and not struggle when problems arise?

I could not enjoy my life.

My actions and attitudes caused me pain.

I became filled with fear.

I felt that I could do nothing.

I was full of gloom and doom.

I was alone.

I was helpless.

I saw that I was the problem.

Then I experienced a moment of clarity.

With courage as my guide I took small steps.

It took a long time to find and accept the God within me.

Once I did the pain, fear, and loneliness I felt was relieved.

That's when my miracle happened.

Things cannot stay the same on our spiritual journey or we won't grow.

We need to uncover – what is blocking us.

Then discover – what actions are needed and take them.

Then discard – what doesn't work for us.

And finally recover – our spiritual well being and spiritual growth.

Forgiveness comes in various forms.

It is in forgiving others.

It is in believing and accepting self forgiveness in our hearts.

It is in the peace we get from knowing God has already forgiven us.

It does not matter in which form forgiveness comes to us first (others, self, God).

What matters is in living life though the practice of forgiveness as we forgive and have been forgiven.

When I am practicing spiritual principles I am less likely to preach, interfere, correct, or criticize someone else's actions.

It is easier in giving suggestions to another person when they directly ask for my help.

I will be far more productive in my efforts when I am giving my experiences and not my opinions.

With these experiences God brings me into a language of the heart.

I am then responsible to pass on that language of the heart, to others, through my actions!

What we are is our gift from God for the world to see.

What we become is our gift back to God and the world that only we see.

Be a comfort to others

Believe that all people are on a spiritual path that brings them closer to God

Know that God is constant

God is my life and He brings us great comfort and peace.

I am on a spiritual journey.

Any roadblocks along the way are opportunities to bring me closer to God.

Guidance isn't telling God to follow your plans.

It is you asking God to show and direct you to His plans and then be willing follow absolutely without reservation.

*When I am grateful you get the best of me,
my time, and my love.*

By staying grateful the world is better place.

*Gratitude is a daily action I take to show
God's presence, qualities, and love working
in my life!*

Be honest…

Be open…

Be willing…

Be still…

Be patient…

Enjoy the moment…

Just be…

Let God do His work!

Worrying about all that we are facing brings us added pressure which makes us ineffective as a result.

Focusing on one thing, setting priorities, and taking action we are often surprised at how much we accomplish and how little we worry!

What does gratitude and forgiveness have in common?

They both free us from self!

One second at a time, one minute at a time, one day at a time, we can accomplish any goal we set for ourselves.

With God's help!

With spirituality as our guide and God in our hearts we are on the right path......

Confront your fears......

There is no better time than now to find out what brings you spiritual growth, joy, and happiness!

Prayer and meditation is a way we feed and take care of our spirit!

Cynicism is doubt always negative expecting the worst......

Faith is trust always positive expecting the best......

Do you know that feeling you have when you feel peace come over you?

When you feel you are one with the world?

When you feel you are filled with a purpose?

Then you know what it is to feel the presence of God!

As I listen, obey, and walk with God may I overcome my selfishness and self-centeredness?

It is not the difficulties that are in my life that I have to overcome.

It is my own selfishness and self-centeredness.

God makes that possible when I listen, obey, and walk with Him!

We can always grow and move forward with help from God!

Sometimes our emotions rule us.

When we are ruled by our emotions we lose sight and become paralyzed with fear.

The knowledge of this does not stop our emotions and fears from over taking us.

It is only when we ask God for help, look inward for understanding, and go to others for guidance that or our paralyzing emotions and fears are relieved!

To say that we don't know something, when you don't know, is always better than pretending that we do know.

Know what I mean?

In our search for happiness, our selfishness and resentments, kept us blocked from God.

No matter what came to us we continued to run on self will and we couldn't find happiness.

We continued to harm ourselves and others.

When we began to seek Gods will and not our will we made progress in overcoming our selfishness and resentments.

We began to help others.

Then our experiences, opportunities, and growth allowed us make better use of our talents and gifts.

We found a new happiness, joy, and freedom knowing God is present in every person and situation!

The cause of today's defects, frustrations, and disappointments can affect you with repeated negativity.

Invest in others through kindness, consideration and love and all that negativity will be overcome.

Sitting and waiting before taking action is based in fear.

As long as the process of making a decision is based in affirmative action through prayer, meditation, and council with others then God will bring you to a place where you can meet Him.

Face your fears and grow into the person
that God wants you to be.

Face your fears to become the person you
never knew you could be.

God loves you and will always be with you to
face your fears.

If you face your fears with God miracles will
happen.

One of the outstanding characteristics of all growth is change......

Reaching out to others with kindness, understanding, compassion and love allows us to be of real service to God and our fellows......

The ability to stop, look, listen, and reflect before taking action is one of the healthiest, and wisest characteristics we can possess on our spiritual journey.

Reflection brings us happiness, joy, freedom, and wealth beyond anything we could imagination!

No matter how much I hide myself from the God within.

I still sense His presence.

Others can sense and see Him too when I stop hiding and allow His love to shine through.

May God inspire, strengthen, and empower you by helping the lives of others through your actions and His continuing grace.

Whenever I am deceiving or misleading I am creating illusions and delusions to myself, others, and God.

Once I surrender to God, admit my faults to others, and accept the truth about myself I once again become a participant in life rather than being isolated and all alone.

No achievement belongs to us alone.

It is comes from the help of others and God.

With their help there is nothing too difficult that cannot be overcome.

That is what fellowship and Love is all about!

The problem with blaming is no one wins and everyone loses!

By restraining from; disrespectful, tactless, selfish, cruel, hurtful, insensitive, callus, inconsiderate, argumentative, forceful, manipulative, self-centered, ad infinitum behaviors......

We are and giving one of the kindest forms of love possible through practicing consideration of others.

God supplies me with all I need.

What more could I possibly ask for?

With God's power in my life my ability to understand many things increases.

Let me stop putting limits on God with my lack of trust, vision, and faith.

Help me keep an open mind to see and embrace all God's influences in my life today.

The expression of love comes in many ways.

One way is by giving love to others in our lives unconditionally.

By giving our love to others unconditionally, do we want anything else?

If we do it's not an expression of love!

When I become willing my mind opens, my ears hear, I pay attention, and then God enters.

Listening to another person's pain, confusion, or fear might make all difference in the world to them.

By giving to others through an open heart and mind and showing acts of kindness, patience, caring, and love.

These are some of the greatest gifts we can give to each other!

Happiness is a byproduct of doing the right thing.

What is the right thing?

Selfless service and love to God and others!

Spirituality is acquired, discovered, experienced, and demonstrated in our lives.

Spirituality is found in and all around us.

The best way to learn about spirituality is to do practice it.

Our job becomes to seek, find, and practice.

I cannot solve anybody's problems.

It's not my place to solve their problems.

It is my place to love, support, encourage and share my experiences as they solve their problems, issues, and situations.

Self deception is nothing more than lying to ourselves.

I have lied to myself so many times without even realizing it.

I used so many excuses to justify my lies.

My deceit was leading me down a path of self destruction.

Then there came a brief fleeting moment of clarity, awareness, and surrender.

I had a new beginning and a way out of the prison called self.

All I had to do was trust in the process, keep doing the work, find God (who wasn't lost), and help others.

I was always either superior or inferior to everybody else.

I was the best or I was not good enough.

I was too good for…… or I was no good at all.

I was worthy or I was unworthy.

I was the best at…. or I don't deserve it.

I was always inflating or degrading myself.

I had no friends because of the way I behaved.

When I realized I was no better and no worse than anyone else, I begin to accept myself.

A wonderful thing happened to me when I stopped trying to be different.

I found balance with God and my fellows.

Balance is found in my relationship with God and my fellows not in being different!

Today we find other ways of dealing with life instead of giving up.

We can remember there are always solutions.

We can ask for help.

We can pray and meditate.

We can take action and make changes.

We can remember with the help of God and others nothing is that overwhelming.

The love and growth of the spiritual process is not based on a matter of success or failure, or is it something that is earned or achieved.

It happens through Gods grace.

Which means it is an unearned gift freely and undeservedly given to us by God!

All the negativity, pain, loss, failures, and heartaches seem to be stopping us from going on.

It seems like our struggles will never end.

When this happens we need a new attitude and a new outlook.

One filled with God, faith, hope, strength, perseverance, patience, acceptance, and love.

Then we no longer have struggles, we just have situations.

When we see others weaknesses we do not confront them instead we talk about our own weaknesses, insecurities, and temptations.

Then we seek and find comfortable ground to communicate and find common solutions.

That's sharing and caring.

Right and wrong is not a mystery to us.

Although we may not always choose to do the right thing we never the less know what the right thing to do should be!

Self will is filled with: fear, doubt, confusion, irritation, pushing, relentlessness, weariness, short - temperedness, rushing, struggling, despairing, criticizing, and irrationality.

Gods will is filled with love.

Which one will I chose today?

It was hard to realize we could not run our own life.

We had to admit, adjust, and accept the idea if we kept running our own life we would keep having problems and troubles.

When we took action by asking for help something began to happen.

We stopped depending on ourselves and started to trust others.

Through the trust of others we were introduced to a Power that began working in our life.

As we trusted that Power more, our problems and troubles seemed to dissipate.

We were no longer running our own life.

We had a new Power and that Power is God!

Our spiritual journey is connected to many others.

We do not do it alone.

Some people help us on our path, while others seem to hurt us.

We don't always understand what part others play.

God places others on our path to help us, even those we believe are hurting us teach us.

Our spiritual journey is always based in God, others, and self.

When we are struggling for power we are managing, controlling, and manipulating.

The more we engage in this struggle the more energy that is taken out of us.

The more energy is taken out of us the greater our frustrations.

The greater our frustrations the more we have expectations.

The more we have expectations the more we struggle for power.

When we stop this self defeating behavior everything starts to change.

We find peace, tranquility, joy, happiness, and freedom.

So why do we struggle for power in the first place?

Meditation looks hard or impossible to achieve.

When we reflect on easy and difficult, beginnings and endings, happiness and sadness, pain and healing we are meditating.

Meditation is not hard or impossible.

Practicing it is!

Our spiritual growth comes from God through the experiences, guidance, and love of those who have gone before us!

Things are never quite what they seem.

The more I think I know the more I do not know or understand.

When I think I have something figured out it changes.

My life is no longer something to be endured, figured out, or tolerated.

When I accept these facts my life becomes a wonderful adventure!

Having serenity with ourselves and peace with others takes time.

We get there by:

Trusting in the process

Having the courage to face life on life's terms

Having faith

Letting go of the past

Believing God loves us

The forgiveness of self and others

Helping others

When we focus on others and want them to change we put conditions on them.

We are really trying to control and manage them.

We then put our own peace, happiness, joy, and serenity in jeopardy.

When we detach and let others be themselves we can still care about them.

We can still pray and wish the best for them.

We can let them be themselves.

We can let go of our control and managing of them.

We can practice unconditional love.

There is no better peace, happiness, joy, and serenity then the practice of unconditional love!

We must not get to confident or comfortable about where we are on our spiritual journey.

We must not allow our past or present achievements fool us into relaxing.

We must not allow complacency or procrastination keep us from taking appropriate actions.

We need to watch out for the dangers of pride, arrogance, and fear.

We need to be vigilant in all we do on our spiritual journey.

Then we need to share our journey with others if we are to continue growing spiritually.

Pain, criticism, self-pity, injustice, hate, resentment, rejection, and fear past and present keep us focused on our negativism.

We change this negative pattern through surrender, prayer, and positive action.

We ask for help in prayer.

We ask the guidance of others.

We become ready and willing to take positive action.

Through the actions we take our perceptions change.

We change from being negative to becoming positive.

The miracle happened!

When we say or commit to doing things regardless of whatever they may be and we go and do them to the best of our ability......

We learn the ability to fulfill our commitments.

We learn we can do what we say.

We learn we can be trustworthy.

We learn we can be honorable.

We learn we have integrity.

We learn we feel good about ourselves.

So why do we procrastinate?

There are recurring thoughts in life.

There are recurring decisions in life.

There are recurring choices in life.

There are recurring actions in life.

There are recurring changes in life.

Over and over until our spiritual lessons are learned!

Life is continuously changing.

With change we get a chance for growth.

With change we are encouraged to take risks.

With change we develop opportunities to learn from our successes and failures.

With change we lose our fear.

With change we gain courage.

With change we are never static.

With change we find hope, faith, and love.

Change is good for us.

So why do we resist life's changes?

Hurt feelings causes us to react and not to respond in a certain way to situations, circumstances, people, and life based on our emotions instead of our intellect......

Through prayer and meditation we grow spiritually.

Communication is prayer.

Listening is meditation.

Spiritually is God.

Simple!

Healthy relationships are based in honesty, openness, trust, consideration, adaptability, communication, balance, forgiveness, courage, faith, belief, awareness, giving, understanding, acceptance, humility, love, ad infinitum.

They are hard work!

When we share the qualities of healthy relationships without reservations and unconditionally we are living in God's will.

Maybe we never learned how to ask for help.

Maybe we never learned how to accept help.

Maybe we believed we should not rely on others for help.

Maybe we believed we should not accept or receive help.

Maybe we believed that strength means we can do it ourselves.

Maybe we needed to change these faulty beliefs.

There is no maybe about it.

We needed to do something.

Through God's help our perceptions, fears, and insincerities began to change.

We got the help from others and gave it too as we are able to ask, perceive, accept, believe, rely, learn, receive, do, and get our strength from God!

We all have been through a lot.

We all lived in pain, hopelessness, and fear.

We can wallow in our past and feel bad.

The bad things from the past cannot change or go away.

What we can change is our prospective and attitude.

When we change our prospective and attitude something happens.

Our past pain, hopelessness, fears, and bad feelings change and we can move forward.

As we move forwarded and give our past to God for His healing we find acceptance.

The change in our prospective, attitude, and acceptance comes from God!

God's work can be seen every time we are touched by someone and every time we touch someone else!

We are powerless over many things.

We are not powerless over our actions, attitudes, commitments, and behaviors.

By taking responsibility and appropriate actions for all we do we are strengthened.

That strength comes from God.

For without the strength from God we would rationalize, minimize, and deceive ourselves right back into total powerlessness.

Today through God I will recommit to responsibilities and appropriate actions.

With God walking with us we need have no fear.

By turning to God for guidance He enables us to explore our strengths and weaknesses.

In this process God shows us there are many things we thought we were incapable of.

One thing we found that we never thought was possible for us was a full and meaningful relationship with God.

With that anything is possible!